AMAZING BRAIN
MYSTERIES

by Cynthia O'Brien

Crabtree Publishing Company
www.crabtreebooks.com

Crabtree Publishing Company
www.crabtreebooks.com

Author: Cynthia O'Brien
Project Editor: Tim Cooke
Designer: Lynne Lennon
Picture Researcher: Andrew Webb
Picture Manager: Sophie Mortimer
Art Director: Keith Davis
Editorial Director: Lindsey Lowe
Children's Publisher: Anne O'Daly
Editor: Kelly Spence
Proofreader: Kathy Middleton
Cover Design: Margaret Amy Salter
Production Coordinator and
    Prepress Technician: Ken Wright
Print Coordinator: Margaret Amy Salter

Photographs
Cover: Shutterstock
Interior: Alamy: Classic Image 13, Mary Evans Picture Library 26, Antony Nettle 19; Corbis: Joel Sartore 25; Getty Images: Barcroft Media 28, Lionel Bonaventure/AFP 29; Kobal Collection: Columbia 10; Library of Congress: 12; Shutterstock: 4, 9, 15, 17, 23, Olga Besnard 7, Stephen Coburn 5, Benjamin Haas 13, Ralph Loesche 16, Pressmaster 22, Paul Vasarhelyi 14, Sorin Vidis 18; Thinkstock: Ana Blazic 11, Lili Graphie 27, istockphoto 6, 8, 20, Baris Urunlu 21, Wavebreak Media Ltd 24.

Every attempt to contact copyright holders has been made by the publisher.

Library and Archives Canada Cataloguing in Publication

O'Brien, Cynthia (Cynthia J.), author
    Amazing brain mysteries / Cynthia O'Brien.

(Mystery files)
Includes index.
Issued in print and electronic formats.
ISBN 978-0-7787-8070-0 (bound).--ISBN 978-0-7787-8074-8 (pbk.).--
ISBN 978-1-4271-9967-6 (pdf).--ISBN 978-1-4271-9963-8 (html)

    1. Brain--Juvenile literature. 2. Memory--Juvenile literature.
I. Title.

QP376.O37 2015   j612.8'2   C2014-908103-0
                                    C2014-908104-9

Library of Congress Cataloging-in-Publication Data

O'Brien, Cynthia (Cynthia J.)
  Amazing brain mysteries / Cynthia O'Brien.
      pages cm. -- (Mystery files)
  Includes index.
  ISBN 978-0-7787-8070-0 (reinforced library binding : alk. paper) --
ISBN 978-0-7787-8074-8 (pbk. : alk. paper) --
ISBN 978-1-4271-9967-6 (electronic pdf : alk. paper) --
ISBN 978-1-4271-9963-8 (electronic html : alk. paper)
  1. Brain--Miscellanea--Juvenile literature. 2. Brain--Physiology--Miscellanea--Juvenile literature. I. Title.

  QP376.O27 2015
  612.8'2--dc23
                                   2014047595

Crabtree Publishing Company
www.crabtreebooks.com   1-800-387-7650

Published in Canada
Crabtree Publishing
616 Welland Ave.
St. Catharines, ON
L2M 5V6

Published in the United States
Crabtree Publishing
PMB 59051
350 Fifth Avenue, 59th Floor
New York, New York 10118

Published by CRABTREE PUBLISHING COMPANY in 2015
Copyright © 2015 Brown Bear Books Ltd

In Canada: We acknowledge the financial support of the Government of Canada through the Canada Book Fund for our publishing activities.

Printed in Canada/022015/MA20150101

Contents

Introduction

The human brain is the body's control center. It keeps us breathing, even when we are asleep. It warns us of danger or makes us feel safe. Your brain signals when you are in pain or when you are hungry. It is where we take in new information. It also controls our **emotions** and holds our thoughts, dreams, and memories. But the brain is also highly mysterious. Sometimes it seems to play tricks, as if there are parts of the brain we cannot control. It causes nightmares, makes people behave in extreme ways, or leaves them unable to recognize familiar people or objects.

An **MRI** scan allows researchers to observe activity in different parts of the brain.

The brain is also capable of remarkable **feats**. Some people claim it can even control objects. Scientists are trying to understand how the brain works. They use powerful scanners to look inside the brain to see what parts are active during activities such as speaking and running. Scientists are constantly discovering the talents of the human brain.

Brain Mysteries

In this book, you will learn about some mysteries of the brain. Read about how experiencing a sense of anxiety has saved people's lives. Learn what people on the very edge of death remember about their experiences. And meet the man who memorized the value of pi—the relationship between the diameter of a circle and its circumference—to over 22,000 decimal places!

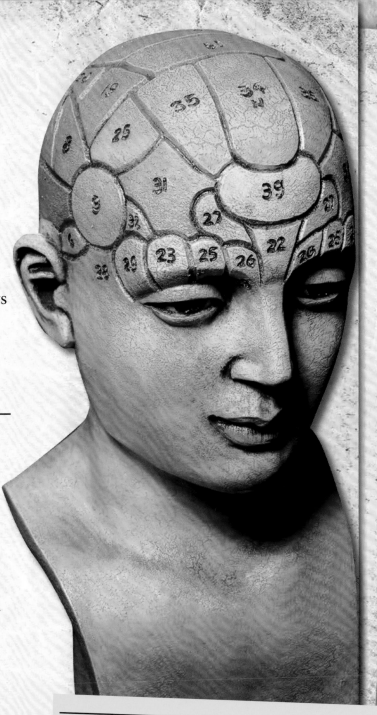

Regions of the brain are mapped and numbered on this model used by medical students.

The Missing
90 PERCENT

The theory that we only use 10 percent of our brains has been around for 100 years. It suggests we have unused powers. However, science has proven this theory is a myth. We use all areas of the brain in our daily lives.

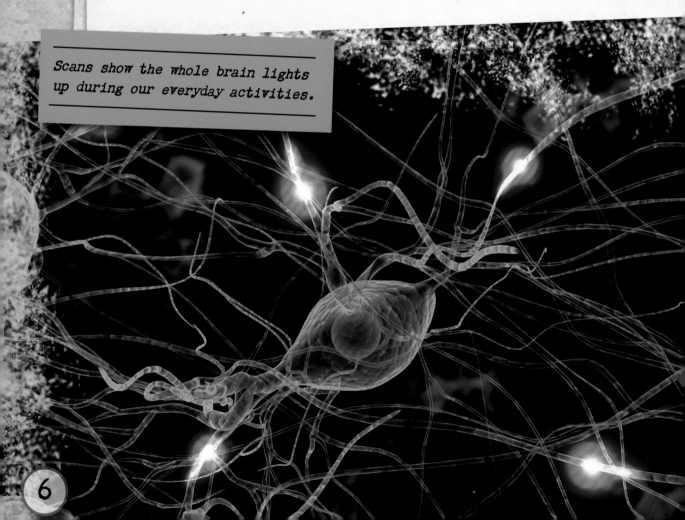

Scans show the whole brain lights up during our everyday activities.

Another myth is that people who use the right side of their brains more are more creative and artistic, and people who are more left-brained are good at math and remembering things. A study of 1,000 brains found that everyone uses both sides of their brain equally.

The right side of the brain controls the left side of the body. The left side of the brain controls the right.

An adult brain weighs about 3 pounds (1.4 kg). It contains billions of **neurons**, or nerves, that use about 20 percent of the body's energy. Even a simple activity like making a sandwich uses many parts of the brain.

Communicating Cells

Scientists who study the brain are called neuroscientists. They have discovered that different parts of the brain control different things. For example, the front left side of the brain controls speech. But mysteries about the structure of the brain still remain. Where does the brain store memories, for example? And how does the brain generate individual feelings, such as love, anger, and sadness?

Mystery words...

neurons: special cells that transmit nerve signals

How Memory
WORKS

Memory is the brain's way of storing and recalling information. This ability is not just for passing a test at school. Everyday activities, such as tying a shoelace or eating a meal, rely on memory.

The brain's billions of neurons make connections as we learn new things. These things are stored as short-term or long-term memories. Short-term memory stays in the mind just long enough to be usable. If we need the information again, our brains store it in the long-term memory.

Most people remember objects and sensations from childhood. These memories are kept in your long-term memory.

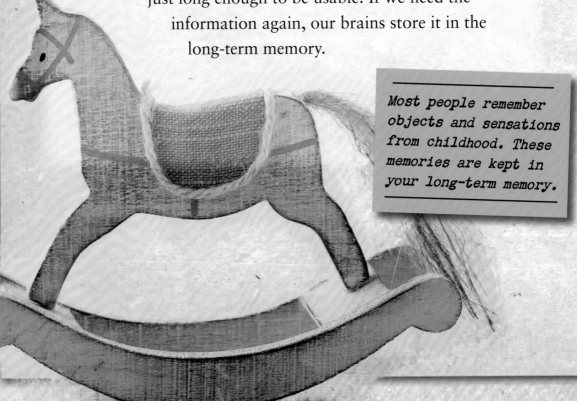

The Hippocampus

How the memory works is a mystery, but scientists do know the **hippocampus** plays an important role. This part of the brain helps to form new memories. It also links memories to emotions and senses.

Sometimes aging causes memory loss. Information does not transfer to the long-term memory. Many older people lose their memories as their neurons lose connections, but scientists do not understand why.

Contestants at the World Memory Championships use a method that turns names, numbers, and facts into pictures. The mind places the images in familiar locations. The mind then "walks" through this place and remembers the image and the original facts.

Experts use special techniques to store and recall memories.

Déjà VU

B I L L M u r r a y

He's having the day of his life...
over and over again.

Groundhog Day

COLUMBIA PICTURES PRESENTS
A TREVOR ALBERT PRODUCTION A HAROLD RAMIS FILM BILL MURRAY ANDIE MacDOWELL
"GROUNDHOG DAY" CHRIS ELLIOTT MUSIC GEORGE FENTON EDITOR PEMBROKE J. HERRING
DESIGNER DAVID NICHOLS DIRECTOR JOHN BAILEY, A.S.C. EXECUTIVE C. O. ERICKSON
STORY DANNY RUBIN SCREENPLAY DANNY RUBIN AND HAROLD RAMIS COLUMBIA PICTURES
PRODUCED TREVOR ALBERT AND HAROLD RAMIS DIRECTED HAROLD RAMIS
PG PARENTAL GUIDANCE SUGGESTED

Have you ever felt as if you have seen or done something before but you know you have not? This strange sensation is called *déjà vu*, which is French for "already seen."

A French philosopher named Emile Boirac first used the term déjà vu in 1876. Since then, people have tried to explain what it means. Some people believe it is a **paranormal** ability that cannot be explained. Déjà vu is difficult to study because it happens quickly and without warning.

In Groundhog Day (1993), Bill Murray plays a man stuck repeating the same day over and over again.

Mystery words...

paranormal: describes something that cannot be explained by science

The opposite of déjà vu is jamais vu, or "never seen." It happens when people do not recognize familiar situations or objects. Some people experience jamais vu after a brain seizure, or spasm. The reasons for the seizures remain a complete mystery.

Over a third of all people say they have experienced déjà vu.

Scientists do have some theories about déjà vu. One is that the brain recalls an old memory that overlaps with a new experience. This makes it seem as though things have happened before. In reality, only part of the new situation or experience is familiar.

Looking Familiar

The brain uses memory to identify things. Something feels familiar when the brain recalls a memory from its long-term storage. Déjà vu may occur when there is a faulty connection between the short-term memory and this longer-term storage. In other words, the brain mixes up the present and the past.

PREMONITIONS

Is it possible to see into the future? Some people claim to have premonitions, or visions of the future. Other people believe they know when something bad is about to happen. But can they know these things ahead of time?

Abraham Lincoln was shot by an assassin as he watched a play.

There are many stories about people avoiding disaster thanks to an unexplained anxiety attack or uneasy feeling. Some of the stories are about people who escape disasters. There are famous tales of people who decided not to use their tickets for the first voyage of the *Titanic* in 1912. The ship sank. In other examples, people decided not to board airplanes which later crashed. Many premonitions appear as dreams. In one famous case, U.S. president Abraham Lincoln dreamed about his own death in 1865. Days later, he was shot in a theater.

Mystery words...

coincidence: events that seem to be linked but are in fact random

A Special Sense?

Some people believe a "sixth sense" explains how people foretell disaster. Other people say premonitions are just **coincidence**. For example, most flights have landed safely even when people decided against boarding them.

But scientific studies do suggest that the brain might have special powers. One common example is the sense you get when someone is approaching you from behind, or when someone is watching you. Perhaps the brain really can warn us of trouble ahead.

Premonitions can be life saving. On September 11, 2001, a New York businessman claims that he felt uneasy on his way to work in the World Trade Center in New York City. When he returned home, he was horrified to see on TV that the building was under attack by terrorists.

Some passengers claim to have had a bad feeling about the Titanic. More than 1,500 lives were lost when it sank.

Near-Death
EXPERIENCES

About eight million Americans claim to have had a near-death experience. Many people believe these experiences prove there is life after death. Others say they are just unexplained tricks of the mind.

In near-death experiences (NDEs), people who have been close to death recover **consciousness** and remember what happened. They often report seeing a bright light or feeling as if they had been floating above their body. Scientists are unsure why, but they believe these sensations may be caused by a lack of oxygen to the brain, or a surge of brain activity during a tramatic event.

People say they remember watching while other people tried to save them.

Some people describe dying as moving along a tunnel toward a bright light.

The Active Brain

Recently, scientists studied 2,000 patients who had suffered heart attacks and survived. Around 40 percent of the patients reported some kind of near-death experience. The brains of the patients kept working for about three minutes after their hearts stopped beating. If the brain shows activity, that means something must be happening inside it. But does the brain experience a real sensation, or is it just mixed-up signals, like déjà vu?

Mystery File:
EDGE OF DEATH

Quick action can bring a person back to life after their heart stops beating. Doctors use a defibrillator to generate electric shocks to restart the heart. That sends fresh oxygen to the brain. But what happens inside the brain while the heart has stopped?

Mystery words...

consciousness: being aware of and responding to one's surroundings

DREAMS

Everyone dreams for about two hours every night, although we do not always remember our dreams. The brain stays active while the body sleeps. Dreams may be part of how our brain learns new information.

Native Americans weave nets called dreamcatchers to protect them from nightmares.

People usually forget their dreams after they wake up. One way to remember your dreams is to keep a notebook by your bed. Write down any dreams as soon as you are awake. Doing this every day will train your mind to remember dreams in more and more detail.

The strange things that happen in dreams may be symbols of other things in our lives.

We dream during periods of deep sleep, known as rapid eye movement (REM) sleep. In deep sleep, the eyes flicker beneath the eyelids. REM sleep **stimulates** the brain's learning centers. Babies have long stages of REM sleep to help their brains develop properly. Even as adults, people need sleep in order to learn new things.

Remembering Dreams

The brain does not process long-term memories while we sleep. Most people do not remember a dream if it ends before they wake up. If we wake up in the middle of a dream, however, the dream may be stored in our memory, although we might have to deliberately try to recall it.

Mystery words...

stimulates: causes to work in a more active way

Mind over MATTER

Some people believe that by **concentrating** very hard on something the brain can help the body overcome physical pain or make us stronger. Some people claim the **mind** even has the power to move **objects**.

Firewalkers train themselves to walk over flaming coals without harm.

Scientific studies show that the same pathways in the brain become active whether we are actually doing something or just thinking about doing it. That suggests that mental exercise can help us improve at physical tasks, such as playing a sport.

Some people also believe that determination can increase our body's strength or resistance to pain. No one knows quite how the brain is able to do this. It may be connected with control of the body's **nervous system.**

Mystery words...

nervous system: the network of nerve cells that send messages around the bod

Positive Thinking

Positive thinking may help the body achieve remarkable feats. Dutch daredevil Wim Hof, for example, uses deep meditation to withstand extreme cold, such as sitting in ice for an hour.

Doctors are also learning to use the power of the brain. In 2013, a Swedish man became the first person to control an artificial arm with his mind. The arm was attached by **electrodes** to his body's nervous system so the brain could send it instructions.

In 2003 illusionist David Blaine went without food for 44 days in a suspended glass box. He used mind control to suppress his hunger.

Mystery File:
TELEKINESIS

For centuries, people have claimed to be able to move objects with their minds. This is called telekinesis. In the late 20th century, the famous illusionist Uri Geller claimed to use his mind to bend spoons or stop watches. Most people believe telekinesis is just a trick.

What are EMOTIONS?

In the ancient world, people believed emotions began in the heart. Now we know the brain controls our emotions as well as our thoughts. But how are emotions different from reason?

People experience six basic emotions: fear, anger, disgust, surprise, joy, and sadness. Three other common feelings are also often counted as emotions: pride, shame, and guilt.

The brain's **limbic system** processes all emotions. The part of the limbic system that creates fear is the amygdala. In a dangerous situation, the amygdala acts like an alarm bell. It sends signals to the body. The heart beats more rapidly and the muscles tense up.

A child screams in anger. When we are angry, more blood flows to the front of our brain.

The ancient Greeks believed the body contained four humors, or fluids. A healthy body had a balance of two kinds of fluid called bile--black and yellow--as well as blood and phlegm. The Greeks thought too much of one humor caused too much emotion.

The face is one way we communicate our emotions to other people.

Meanwhile, the frontal **cortex**, or outer layer, of the brain, which is necessary for thinking, decides if the situation is actually dangerous. If it isn't, the cortex signals to the amygdala there is nothing to fear, and the body relaxes.

Chemical Messengers

Different chemicals in the brain control our emotions. These chemicals transfer messages between cells and to other areas of the brain. Some of the chemicals stimulate the brain. Dopamine, for example, helps us concentrate on particular tasks. Other chemicals calm the brain. Serotonin is produced when we feel happy.

Mystery words...

limbic system: part of the brain that deals with emotions and urges such as hunger

TWINS

Twins often look alike, and sometimes their minds even seem to have a mysterious connection. Some twins seem to communicate without speaking or over long distances. This bond fascinates scientists. What explains the apparent powers of twins?

Twins do not always react in the same way to a situation.

Identical twins share the same **genes**, and their brains are very similar in structure. However, even the brains of identical twins are very different. No two brains interpret an experience the same way, so even twins who have similar experiences develop different personalities.

Some twins share exactly the same opinions even if they have been raised apart.

Two of a Kind

Studies have found that one in five sets of identical twins and one in ten sets of nonidentical twins claim to have a strange bond. For instance, sets of twins record having similar dreams. Others claim to know when their twin is in pain or to be able to send each other messages with their minds. However, scientists say the close bond between the twins is only part of the explanation. The other part may be coincidence.

Mystery File:
TWINS ON TV

In 2003, a TV show recorded an experiment with twins Richard and Damien Powles. They sat where they could not hear or see each other. Richard plunged his arm into cold water and gasped. At that moment, Damien caught his breath. It was as if he, too, felt the cold water.

HYPNOTISM

Imagine someone else taking control of your body and making you do whatever he or she wants. Some people claim that this is what happens during hypnotism. The person goes into a trance, during which he or she is controlled by the hypnotist.

You may have seen shows in which people are hypnotized. The subjects seem to react to suggestions from the hypnotist. They might behave in a silly way when the hypnotist says a key word, even though they may not know why they are acting strangely.

Stage hypnosis is not all it seems, however. Often the victim is part of the act, or they are people who are most open to the idea of being hypnotized in the first place.

Hypnotists sometimes swing a watch to try to focus a person's eyes.

In fact it is very difficult to hypnotize someone who does not want to be hypnotized. Even a hypnotized person will not do something completely against his or her will.

Useful Hypnosis

Hypnosis can be useful, however. **Psychiatrists** use it help their patients overcome problems. Some people claim hypnotherapy can help people give up smoking or overeating. People also use it to cure **insomnia** and to lessen stress. Could it be that being put into a trance by a medical expert makes the mind more open to the power of suggestion after all?

Mystery File: HYPNOSIS AND MEMORY

Hypnosis may have the power to unlock the memory. People in trances are able to recall information they cannot otherwise remember. Experts are working on how to stop memory loss, or dementia, which often affects older people. It may be that the solution lies in the brain.

Mystery words...

insomnia: a regular inability to sleep

Past LIVES

TRUE STORIES OF THE STRANGE AND THE UNKNOWN

FATE AND MAGAZINE

November 1956

35¢

BRIDEY MURPHY IN IRELAND

A Personal Investigation

By WILLIAM J. BARKER

In the 1950s, a Virginia housewife claimed to have been Bridey Murphy, a woman from 19th-century Ireland.

Under hypnosis, some people tell stories of lives they lived before they were born. Some even seem to speak a different language. Can they really be remembering past lives?

Past-life **regression** claims to help people recall former lives. During this type of hypnosis, our brain waves change from their usual pattern. Some people claim this suggests we enter another state of consciousness that makes it possible to revisit former lives. Another theory for these past-life recollections is that our genes contain memories. This might explain how even some children claim to remember past lives.

Scientific Theories

Quantum mechanics is a type of science that deals with particles smaller than atoms. At that scale, scientists say time and space mingle. Parallel universes, which are realities that exist at the same time, become possible. Time is no longer a simple case of past, present, and future. In this world, consciousness exists outside of the brain. That means the same consciousness could transfer from brain to brain. Scientists are exploring this amazing theory.

A three-year-old American named Hunter believed he was the great 1930s' U.S. golfer Bobby Jones in a past life. He had remarkable golf skills and even designed golf courses. A few years later, the boy's memories of a past life had vanished-- but his golf ability remained.

Is it possible for the mind to "remember" lives from the past?

Mystery words...

regression: a return to a former life or state of being

27

Extraordinary GIFTS

A small group of people with a brain disorder known as savant syndrome have extraordinary gifts in math, music, art, and in memory tasks.

Some people acquire savant syndrome. For example, after 10-year-old Orlando Serrell was struck on the head by a baseball, he could do calendar calculations. He could figure out on which day of the week any date in the future would fall.

Daniel Tammet is a savant who memorized the value of pi to over 22,000 digits.

Savant Syndrome

About half of all savants are also autistic. **Autism** is a condition that makes it difficult for an individual to communicate with and relate to other people.

The link between autism and savants is not understood. In savants, damage in the left brain may cause the rest of the brain to rewire itself. This unlocks skills in the right brain, usually in one area. An autistic brain may be wired in a similar way.

Mystery File:
MASTER DRAWER

British artist Stephen Wiltshire draws cities in amazing detail. This talented savant draws or paints whole cityscapes after looking at a scene for a brief time. Wiltshire is one of just 100 or so diagnosed savants in the world.

Mystery words...

autism: a mental condition that makes it difficult to communicate

Glossary

autism A mental condition that makes it difficult to communicate

coincidence Events that seem to be linked but are in fact random

consciousness Being aware of and responding to one's surroundings

cortex The outer layer of the brain, which plays an important role in consciousness

dementia A persistent loss of memory caused by aging, sickness, or injury

electrodes Conductors through which electricity passes

emotions Strong feelings caused by one's situation, mood, or relationships to other people

feats Achievements that require great courage or skill

genes Chemical units that pass on parents' characteristics to their children

hippocampus A part of the brain responsible for emotions, learning, and memory

hypnotism The deliberate creation of a state in which a subject appears to be in a trance and becomes very open to suggestion

insomnia A regular inability to sleep

limbic system Part of the brain that deals with emotions and drives such as hunger

MRI Magnetic resonance imaging; a technique for scanning body parts

myth An idea that is widely believed but which is false

nervous system The network of nerve cells that send messages around the body

neurons Special cells that transmit nerve signals

paranormal Describes something that cannot be explained by science

psychiatrist An expert in how the mind works and how it affects behavior

premonition A strong feeling that something unpleasant or unwelcome is about to happen

regression A return to a former life or state of being

scan A medical procedure that uses a beam or detector to take a cross-section inside the body

stimulates Causes to work in a more active way

Find Out More

BOOKS

Ballard, Carol. *The Brain and Nervous System* (Exploring the Human Body). KidHaven, 2005.

Brynie, Faith Hickman. *101 Questions Your Brain Has Asked About Itself But Couldn't Answer... Until Now*. Twenty-First Century Books, 2007.

Markle, Susan. *Wounded Brains: True Survival Stories* (Powerful Medicine). Lerner Publishing Group, 2010.

Burstein, John. *The Astounding Nervous System: How Does My Brain Work* (Slim Goodbody's Body Buddies). Crabtree, 2009.

Strange, Christopher M. *The Brain Explained* (The Guide for Curious Minds). Rosen Publishing Group, 2014.

WEBSITES

Brain Mysteries
Five mysteries about the brain, compiled by How Stuff Works.com.
http://science.howstuffworks.com/life/inside-the-mind/human-brain/5-brain-mysteries.htm

More Mysteries
The BBC news website has its own list of unsolved mysteries of the brain.
www.bbc.co.uk/news/health-25462959

Under Hypnosis
How Stuff Works.com explores whether hypnosis actually works.
http://science.howstuffworks.com/science-vs-myth/extrasensory-perceptions/hypnosis.htm

Index